T0343113

the little book of
Tarot

The Tarot feels like talking to an old, wise elder with a wicked sense of humour.

the little book of
Tarot

ELENA ALDEN

GODSFIELD

For Anne

An Hachette UK Company
www.hachette.co.uk

First published in Great Britain in 2023
by Gaia Books, an imprint of Octopus
Publishing Group Ltd
Carmelite House
50 Victoria Embankment
London EC4Y 0DZ
www.octopusbooks.co.uk

This edition published in 2024 by
Godsfield Press, an imprint of Octopus
Publishing Group Ltd

Copyright © Octopus Publishing Group
Limited 2023, 2024

Distributed in the US by
Hachette Book Group
1290 Avenue of the Americas
4th and 5th Floors
New York, NY 10104

Distributed in Canada by
Canadian Manda Group
664 Annette St.
Toronto, Ontario, Canada M6S 2C8

ISBN 978-1-8418-1587-9

A CIP catalogue record for this book is
available from the British Library.

Printed and bound in China
10 9 8 7 6 5 4 3 2 1

Publisher: Lucy Pessell
Designer: Isobel Platt &
Hannah Valentine
Editor: Feyi Oyesanya
Assisant Editor: Samina Rahman
Production Manager: Allison Gonsalves
Illustrations: Barbara Malagoli

Contents

Introducing
the Tarot

If your life feels overwhelming, confusing or stuck, picking up a deck of Tarot cards is one of the most rewarding and creative ways to find answers. Despite its esoteric and sometimes unnerving reputation, Tarot is a friendly and enjoyable way to explore your life's journey, whoever you are and whatever you're dealing with. All you need is curiosity and a willingness to tell the truth.

What if I told you that our lives are made up of a set number of stories or patterns? Each of these stories waxes and wanes throughout our lives, becoming more dominant and less so day by day as our attention, moods and concerns shift and change, but we all have these stories and patterns in common: they are what unite us and make us human.

The Tarot, at its simplest, depicts 78 of these stories. Each story card holds a secret lesson or teaching, and deciphering each card's secret is what reading the Tarot is all about.

Whether these lessons apply to our present, past or future is up to us, but as we are only ever really here, in this moment of time, the Tarot is most useful at helping us see more clearly where we are right now. Rather than 'predicting' the future, by showing us our behaviours, thoughts and blindspots, the Tarot can also help us to see where we might be headed if we don't make a change.

Think of the deck as a wise, no-nonsense friend or therapist, the kind who always seems to know the raw truth behind things, who helps you to see how you could move forward with hope and love rather than shame. You can turn to them every day no matter how you're feeling; they will never judge you and always accept you exactly as you are. I think we're all in need of a friend like that.

The History of the Tarot

Tarot cards are said to trace their meanings and origins back to the late 14th century, but are thought to have their roots in both ancient Egyptian and Greek mysticism. As long as there have been human beings, the wisest ones among us have attempted to depict and code the mysteries and truths of life. Tarot is one of the ways in which this wisdom and life experience have been passed down, with each generation's readers and teachers adding their own new perspectives.

Originally, cards were used that look much like our common playing cards. Divided into four suits – wands, cups, coins and swords – each card had a particular shared meaning associated with it, like a collection of folktales passed from person to person. As time went by, it became the fashion to commission additional 'trump' cards to add to your deck. Drawn by skilled artists, they depicted more universal themes and featured elaborate pictures of archetypal images such as The Fool, Justice, Death, Lovers, a Hanged Man. These more famous cards are likely the ones that you are most familiar with.

It is this evolution that gave Tarot its two main components: the older Minor Arcana with its suits, numbers and court cards, and the newer 22 Major Arcana or trump cards. 'Arcana' means mysteries or secrets. We'll learn more about the difference between these two parts of the deck on pages 46 and 22.

The Tarot deck that you've probably seen most often, and the one on which this Little Book's readings are founded, is the Rider-Waite deck drawn by Pamela Colman Smith. First published in 1909, Smith was the first artist, as far as we know, to introduce iconic characters and scenes into the

Minor Arcana cards, rather than just drawing the trumps, and her colourful and lively deck has become the template on which most modern Tarot decks are based. A resurgence of interest in Tarot in recent times has led to a growing abundance of beautiful and diverse decks for us to own and explore, but Smith's symbolism still runs deep.

Although life has changed considerably over the centuries, the fact that our brains and bodies still work in the same way means that we share a surprising amount in common with people of the past. It is in this way that the Tarot could be said to represent something universal about humanity: the dramas, pain, fears and joys that seem hardwired into us as human beings. It is these archetypes of human experience that make the Tarot as relevant and insightful today as it ever was.

Getting Started

Are you ready to get to know all 78 of these wonderful stories and learn their secrets?

You will need

- A full deck of Tarot cards, preferably the original Rider-Waite deck or one based on its symbolism.

- A notebook and pen.

- Some quiet time, preferably alone when you can think without distraction.

- A curious attitude. Try to drop all judgements and expectations, just for a while.

I also recommend that you take some time to read this Little Book all through so that you can familiarize yourself with its layout and the Tarot structure, get a sense of what to expect, and see where you might find answers to some of your questions.

How to Use Your Cards

Exploring the Cards and Ourselves

Whether or not you've ever looked at Tarot cards before, I encourage you to take your deck and spread out all the cards in front of you. Forget the images you may have in your head of a mysterious, veiled woman laying out cards in a row for an anxious-looking querent. Forget any sense of 'doing a reading' and just look. What do you see?

Do the images on the card make you smile, make your heart beat faster, feel frightening, confusing or daft? There are no wrong answers, but it can be useful to see where you're starting from.

Anxiety

If you feel a sense of threat or worry, chances are that anxiety is going to be a companion in your readings. If you're afraid of change, feel overwhelmed by life or feel like bad news is lurking around every corner, the cards can help you with that. You can bring your anxiety to your readings and know you are safe. There are no nasty surprises waiting here, just a gentle sort of unknotting to help you look at your fears more closely. Tarot can help you look at your influences and inherited stories. See this as your chance to find out for yourself what is actually true for you.

Doubt

If you feel a sense of disconnection or cynicism, chances are that doubt is going to be your companion. That's OK – it's good to not believe everything at face value! The Tarot will allow you to be discerning and analytical, and test its theories. If you're put off by the pictures, remember that they are just symbols. See them as something neutral that you can interpret however you want.

Whatever you feel, write it out like this:

'I feel [name your feeling].This means that [name a state of mind] is going to be with me as I read the cards.'

Cognitive Bias

This simple first exercise is a quick and helpful way to see what expectations, wounds and hang-ups you bring with you to your card readings. It will affect what conclusions you jump to, what you filter out and what you focus on. It is your own personal cognitive bias and is likely to make you more reactive or defensive to things that touch on it. You don't need to change how you feel or be ashamed of it – we all have biases – but if you can spot this from the start, it will be easier to see when something is getting in the way of your readings, obscuring a wider view or new perspective.

Because our biases often shift and change depending on the concerns of the day, I recommend checking in with your biases regularly.

EXERCISE:
A Card a Day

The best way to get to know the cards and incorporate Tarot into your life is to pick one card to focus on each day. The ideal time to do this is in the morning so you can reflect on the card as the day unfolds.

A daily practice:

1. Give your deck a good shuffle so that both the Major and Minor Arcana cards are all mixed up together.

2. Close your eyes and take a few slow breaths until you feel still and calm.

3. Ask a question, in your head or out loud. I suggest: 'What do I need to see more clearly today?'

4. Spread out the cards with their backs to you, in your hands or on a table.

5. With your eyes closed, begin to touch the cards until your fingers settle on one. Pull it out and look at it.

6. Jot down your immediate reactions and associations. What thoughts and mental pictures does this card spark? How do you feel? Write this down before looking up the meaning of the card.

7. Turn to the card's listing in this Little Book to deepen your exploration.

8. Use the template below to gather together your final thoughts:

• My card today is: _____

• It feels relevant because: _____

• I feel confused about: _____

• I might be biased toward focusing on: _____

• Perhaps I also need to think about: _____

• My gut instinct tells me it could also mean: _____

• In response today, I would like to: _____

About the Card Interpretations

An interpretation of each of the Major and Minor Arcana cards is listed in the following chapters to guide your practice, but think of them as prompts rather than rules. As you read my words, what new trains of thought start to run through your mind? Look at the card again. Know that there is a story about your unique life hidden inside it. My learning and understanding come from seeing through the lens of my own life, but your life will be different. What personal wisdom and experience can you bring to the table?

Cards Representing Other People

You will notice that I have deliberately kept each card interpretation focused on you. This is because you are the only person whose life and choices you have full control over. It is always wisest to prioritize insight into your own nature rather than trying to second-guess other people (who you can't change anyway). That being said, our lives are interwoven with others and Tarot can act as a useful window to help you see people's patterns and behaviours from a new perspective. When you draw a card, it's worth thinking about who else the figure or figures depicted might represent. Still, remember to look with eyes of empathy rather than judgement. We all hold aspects of all of the cards. Let other people act as a mirror for your own self-learning.

Feeling Unsafe

Do some of the cards scare you? It's important to stress that there are no bad cards in Tarot. As you get to know them, you'll start to learn that even startling cards like Death or The Tower aren't as frightening or foreboding as you might think. If you get a sudden clench of fear, take a deep breath and remind yourself that nothing has gone wrong. However, if you find any cards to be so triggering as to cause you distress or severe anxiety, just take those cards out of the deck for a while and work with the others until you feel ready to add the triggering cards back.

Tarot for Guidance and Clarity

In our daily practice, I have suggested, 'What do I need to see more clearly today?' as a question to ask, but of course you can ask any question of the cards.

Here are some other questions to try:

- What insight could help me with [state your situation]?

- I'm feeling [state your feeling]. What extra information do I need to help me make a good choice today?

- I'm obsessing about [state your thoughts]. What would help me see the bigger picture?

Spend some time making a list of questions you could ask.

Reverse Meanings

You may have seen reference to 'reversed' cards. This is when you draw and place a Tarot card down on a surface in front of you and see that you've placed it upside down. With a well-shuffled deck, this happens all the time. Some Tarot books even come with a whole secondary encyclopaedia of reverse meanings. Do you need to try and learn them, too?

The answer is, simply, that it's up to you. You can think of reversed cards as a kind of expansion pack for your Tarot practice: entirely optional, but interesting if you want to continue to explore Tarot in new ways.

A reversed card in your draw could mean:

- The polar opposite of the normal interpretation: literally the picture or story turned on its head. What might the opposite meaning be?

- An unexpected element, one that will make you feel especially uprooted.

- This is a card that you're particularly resistant to. What do you need to do to turn the card the right way up in your life?

- Something isn't quite what it seems and requires deeper reflection.

If you'd like to work with reversals, I have provided a question prompt for each card to get you started, but I encourage you to use your own intuition too. What darker or more obscured truth might be trying to get your attention?

The Major Arcana

These bold cards depict life's biggest, most transformative lessons. Spread out the Major Arcana cards in order and read their descriptions and you may perceive a linear sequence or story line running through them.

The Major Arcana depicts an archetypal quest, much like the one described by American writer Joseph Campbell in The Hero with a Thousand Faces – an analysis of the various stages of the classic hero's journey – with The Fool acting as the fresh-faced protagonist heading out the door to learn something new.

Imagine The Fool meeting each lesson in turn, being changed by it, growing and maturing a little with each card. We are The Fool, of course, and our life's path will lead us through iterations of this journey many times. Sometimes these first 22 cards are described as a circle: the revelations of The World lead us right back to start as The Fool again, new, wiser, changed. I like to think of this cycle as a spiral, each turn leading me deeper and deeper.

When you draw a Major Arcana card in your reading, it's time to think about where in this cycle of growth you might find yourself right now. Perhaps your card is the lesson you most need to work with and integrate next to help you find the freedom to move forward with your life.

0: The Fool

Begin again.

In order for our lives to change and grow, we must embrace being a beginner again. This means taking a risk that you'll look stupid, fail or get it wrong, but this is how we shake things up. It means accepting that you can't get from here to there in one leap. There will need to be many patient steps, highs and lows. The rest of the Tarot teaches how to manage the journey ahead of you. The Fool is your first nudge out the door; the call to a new adventure. Embrace the chance to start fresh.

Keywords: beginnings, risk, childlike-optimism, spontaneity, faith, boldness, adventure, possibility

Reversed Card Question:
'What does staying stuck help me to avoid?'

1: The Magician

Use what you have.

Another word for The Magician is 'alchemist'. This is deep creativity, turning the raw stuff of life into something new. The Magician holds all the tools of the Tarot – thoughts, feelings, energy and hard work – and knows that together they can make powerful things happen. Today, don't wait for life to give you what you want. Create it yourself. Look at what's available to you. True creativity is about working inventively with what you have, yourself included. Anything is possible with enough patience, focus and experimentation.

Keywords: action, pragmatism, resourcefulness, creativity, power, self-sufficiency, manifestation, focus, alchemy, problem-solving

Reversed Card Question:
'I might be saying the right things and putting on a good show, but am I taking any real action?'

The Magician

2: The High Priestess

Make space and listen.

What would it mean to really listen? We can be so busy talking, using our words and bodies to make sure we don't disappear,that we can fill up life with our own noise. When we choose to be quiet, we make space. Here's a chance to hear new and different voices: the quieter voice of your intuition, the wisdom of teachers, the mysterious messages of nature. What happens when you accept that you don't know all the answers; when you don't rush to fill all spaces? Be still. Listen to what speaks up when you stop.

Keywords: wisdom, intuition, authenticity, solitude, silence, mystery, meditation, stillness, patience, guidance

Reversed Card Question:
'What am I refusing to do that I know, deep down, is right?'

The High Priestess

3: The Empress

Be in your body.

We're encouraged to live in our heads, always thinking, planning, assessing. What's below our neck is either an afterthought or something to be resented and tightly controlled. When we pay attention to our body, allowing it freedom to move and feel just as it is, we gain access to a vital creative power. Today, feel your feet on the ground. Spend time outside. Connect with your sensuality, the instincts that come from your skin and your gut. Think about what it means to be wild. How might it change you to live this way? To completely inhabit your body, however imperfect it is?

Keywords: nature, self-love, self-care, sensuality, creativity, self-expression, connection, compassion, pleasure, freedom

Reversed Card Question:
'If I knew I wouldn't be judged for it, I would love to...'

4: The Emperor

Take charge.

Authority is rarely comfortable. Sometimes we must step up, take control of our own lives and make decisions that affect others. These moments don't come when things feel easy. They happen when the stakes are high. Often we don't feel ready. Still, we must sit up tall in this hard, uncomfortable place and speak with strength and cool, calm conviction. Yes, you might feel scared. Yes, it might cause conflict. Authority is about having the wisdom and courage to know that you need to act anyway. You can hold all these feelings and still do the right thing.

Keywords: power, control, responsibility, self-worth, leadership, truth, courage, empowerment, assertion, action

Reversed Card Question:
'What helps to shake me out of victim-thinking?'

5: The Hierophant

Ask big questions.

The Hierophant holds a double invitation. The first is to examine your influences. What experiences have shaped your beliefs and values? Whose rules are you following and what do you find yourself joining in with? Is this deepening your connection to the world and others or closing your mind? The second invitation is to cut out the middleman. Maybe you could explore and open directly to something bigger than you. What does it mean to accept that you're not the highest power in the universe? What if you tried seeking out this 'something bigger?' What might it teach you?

Keywords: influences, beliefs, teachings, tradition, religion, ideology, conformity, divinity, faith, spirituality

Reversed Card Question:
'What effect do my beliefs have on the way I treat other people?'

The Hierophant

6: The Lovers

Explore loving behaviours.

To love someone well is a choice we must keep making. We make choices day to day based on old dynamics and beliefs that can stretch right back to our childhood. This is how we perpetuate patterns in our lives. Use this card as a prompt to look at your relationships. Are you reacting in the same way over and over, wondering why nothing changes? Or is your pattern to sabotage, cheat, fantasize or run away as a way to avoid dealing with real life? As well as choosing love and care over dysfunction, you can also choose to change the pattern.

Keywords: relationships, love, emotion, choice, connection, commitment, attraction, chemistry, communication

Reversed Card Question:
'Am I truly being loving here, or just trying to get my own way?'

7: The Chariot

Accept your personal power.

Let's talk about willpower. The Serenity Prayer says, 'grant me the serenity to accept the things I cannot change, courage to change the things I can, and wisdom to know the difference'. This is The Chariot. As life races us along, willpower can be an incredible tool to help us 'course correct' and move us closer to what we want. It can also be a tremendous source of frustration and wasted energy. We can't control everything. When would it be wise to exert some willpower today and when do you need to let go?

Keywords: willpower, control, force, movement, change, triumph, grit, wisdom, strength, mastery

Reversed Card Question:
'What same obstacles do I keep hitting?'

The Chariot

8: Strength

Help yourself to feel safe.

We all have impulses and behaviours that cause
problems. True strength isn't about force – it's a
softer, wiser kind of self- management. It's the
strength to do what's right, to take care of yourself
knowing that your wellbeing has an impact on
others, and to see when you're doing things that
aren't in your best interest. Giving yourself a hard
time isn't going to help; change only comes when
we feel safe. Your job is to make sure you're talking
to yourself with love and support so that you feel
safe enough to make different, better choices.

Keywords: non-violence, self-compassion, healing,
patience, gentleness, sensitivity, acceptance,
responsibility, safety, love

Reversed Card Question:
*'How am I sending myself
the message that I'm still not
good enough?'*

9: The Hermit

Make the most of solitude.

Being alone can feel like a punishment, rejection.
Or maybe you're someone who pulls solitude around
you like a wall, to keep everyone and everything
out. The Hermit suggests a wiser way to frame being
alone—retreat not as avoidance or punishment but as
something deep and fruitful. Turn toward solitude
today as away to let the jumble stillness, like a clear
pool. Lean on the things that give you strength to
hold you steady as you watch, feel, learn. There is a
breakthrough to be found here.

Keywords: introspection, solitude, inner-wisdom,
study, insight, retreat, focus, truth, meditation

Reversed Card Question:
*'What am I trying to
avoid feeling?'*

10: The Wheel of Fortune

Keep going.

We love life when it's going well and hate when it isn't. The Wheel of Fortune reminds us that it's all one big endless cycle, as natural as the turning of the seasons. Change is going to happen whether you fight it or not, so why not use your energy for other things? While your life ebbs and flows, you have the option to just quietly get on with what matters to you, on good days and bad. Trust that the wheel will turn again and again and you'll be OK. In the meantime, choose to be your own steady, consistent power and keep working with what you've got.

Keywords: seasons, change, time, luck, resilience, faith, positivity, flexibility, impermanence

Reversed Card Question:
'What step could I take today to change my fate?'

The Wheel of Fortune

11: Justice

Steer toward the good.

Justice is a loaded, heavy word. How about balance? There are patterns and energies that run through life that are hard to notice. We do this, and that happens, someone else does that and this happens. How is this kind of cause and effect showing up in your life right now? Like it or not, we are all beings of action: everything we do and say triggers new chains of consequence and reaction. Whatever is happening, you can always decide to do something different, to set a new pattern in motion. We all have the power to make the world better, or worse.

Keywords: choices, karma, power, responsibility, fairness, morality, balance, consequences, values

Reversed Card Question:
*'What practical thing could I do
instead of blaming or complaining?'*

12: The Hanged Man

Wait and see.

Sometimes the best thing is to simply wait. Feeling trapped is painful but things often just need more time. Accepting what is happening will feel uncomfortable. Your instinct will be to tense up, react, struggle, to try and fix things to make any bad feelings go away. In meditation, we call this 'holding your seat' – it's about staying put, riding waves of thought, feeling and sensation. Today, just notice how you feel, your thoughts coming and going, any tension in your body. Breathe through it. Just wait. Trust that things are changing even if you can't see it.

Keywords: stillness, endurance, acceptance, patience, surrender, rest, restriction, calm, discomfort, stasis

Reversed Card Question:
'Is change actually possible here?
What's patience and what's denial?'

13: Death

Become something new.

We all know death to be an ending, but Tarot teaches us a deeper truth. Death tells us that we must all change form many times. Our existence is always in motion and we don't get to hold anything still or unchanging for long. What is changing for you right now? You might feel grief, liberation, horror, relief, shock, panic. All feelings are valid. There is no easy answer here. No quick fix. Just honour what you must let go, and, when you're ready, try to open, gently, to what your new form might be next. Think of caterpillars and butterflies.

Keywords: change, renewal, loss, endings, beginnings, resistance, freedom, release, transformation

Reversed Card Question:
'What idea or memory do I keep clinging to?'

14: Temperance

Choose the middle way.

Forever thinking in extremes – good/bad, all/nothing, this/not that – is how we keep ourselves stuck. It can lead us to make judgemental choices, make us feel powerless or drive deep wedges of division between us. He should...I can't...She never... Where are strong words like this showing up in your life? Think of this card as a kind of softening, the middle way between extremes. What if everything wasn't as absolute as you think? Maybe it's time to experiment with a new way of doing things: one that holds a bigger, saner picture of possibility.

Keywords: balance, fairness, non-judgement, compassion, humility, moderation, patience, healing, compromise

Reversed Card Question:
'What am I convinced I'm right about? What if I'm not?'

15: The Devil

Notice what controls you.

We all have things we cling to even if they hurt us. Habits, beliefs, addictions, obsessions. It's a hard truth: the things that feel most comforting aren't necessarily helping you. It takes strength to look at your thoughts, patterns and coping strategies and to see that they're keeping you trapped, but there's a big, fresh world out there and it's calling you home. Are you thinking, reacting and behaving as the person you most aspire to be? The rest of your life is still one big possibility. Own up. Ask for help so you can learn how to make changes. Start today.

Keywords: addiction, delusion, self-deception, self-sabotage, passivity, self-destruction, victimhood, dependence, liberation

Reversed Card Question:
'What excuses do I keep making?'

16: The Tower

Trust in change.

Change is frightening. We know it can come out of nowhere, pulling out the ground from beneath us, but this card isn't a portent of doom – it's simply a nudge to notice how anxious you feel about things that are uncertain. A lot of anxiety comes from us feeling sure there is only one right story and that anything else happening would be a disaster. What if that's not true? What if the tower is asking you to trust? Maybe life won't go as you've planned but you'll still be OK. Can you try on that thought today?

Keywords: upheaval, uncertainty, trust, possibility, revelation, catastrophizing, assumptions, hope, breakthrough, awakening

Reversed Card Question:
'What story do I keep telling myself about the future?'

17: The Star

Seek out inspiration.

Having wishes and goals means having hope, but hope doesn't grow out of dry ground. When we feel hopeless, empty or uninspired, we need to seek out things that might help restore our sense that good things are possible. The Star represents everything that can rekindle a fresh sense of optimism, inspiration and creative drive. What do you need to start dreaming again? A change of scene? To try something new? Seek out things to nourish and stimulate you.

Keywords: inspiration, hope, renewal, creativity, dreams, energy, meaning, purpose, motivation

Reversed Card Question:
'What do I keep saying no to?
What if I said yes?'

19: The Moon

Embrace not knowing everything.

Nothing in life can be fully understood and rationalized, however much we try to control it. There are mysteries and hidden sides to all things, ourselves included. It is this deep, pulling well of unsettling feelings, thoughts, and energy that can make us feel off-kilter, wild, even afraid. Instead of seeing the unknowable as an enemy to be feared, fought or repressed, could you see it as an ally? What if you relaxed and opened up to things being a mystery? Let go of your need to jump to conclusions, define or explain everything and just see what happens, what shifts and changes.

Keywords: fears, mysteries, instinct, thoughts, anxiety, confusion, repression, projection, dreams

Reversed Card Question:
'What am I afraid is true?
What am I afraid is not true?'

19: The Sun

Practise joy.

Feeling joy takes practice. If we're not careful, cynical or negative thought patterns, anxiety or constantly craving more can leave us unable to enjoy what's right in front of us. For joy to find us, we need to find ways to accept and welcome things as they are. This starts with seeing ourselves and our muddles with good humour – it's all OK. Next, look up. What's here? However we're feeling, we can always choose to embrace pleasure, beauty, playfulness. The best thing is, if you let the sun's energy in, it will start to shine out of you, too. Joyful people are a gift to the world.

Keywords: joyfulness, action, vitality, energy, gratitude, play, optimism, positivity, celebration

Reversed Card Question:
'What things feed and reinforce a sense of misery in my life?'

20: Judgement

Try on a new attitude.

The surprise in this card is that it's about resurrection. A new start. And right now, the only person who is judging you and holding you back from a new life is you! Self-criticism can be the biggest barrier to our growth, keeping us small. When we repeat the message that we're not good enough, we end up turning away from opportunities that could change our life. The Judgement card asks you to look honestly at yourself. Are all these 'facts' about yourself true, or just old stories? If they're just old stories, maybe it's time to start writing a new one?

Keywords: self-honesty, change, rebirth, growth, healing, transformation, self-help, introspection, action

Reversed Card Question:
'What am I most defensive about?
What fear hides beneath it?'

21: The World

Celebrate the bigger picture.

Other Tarot cards help us pull out a single thread to look at, but The World card is the cloth: all truths, all existence, everything, all at once. Today, try to catch a glimpse of this big, glorious picture. See where you are, how far you've come and all you have yet to learn. Embrace all of it. You are the story of the universe itself. Let your mind and heart be as expansive as it is. 'There is even more to this than I can see.' Say it with relief. Say it with exhilaration. Life is big and that is wonderful.

Keywords: wholeness, perspective, expansion, complexity, completion, celebration, wisdom, non-duality, peace

Reversed Card Question:
'What are all the things that feel true to me right now even if they seem to contradict each other?'

The Minor Arcana

The cards of the Minor Arcana show us the stuff of everyday: the stresses, activities, celebrations and concerns that ebb and flow throughout our ordinary lives. The cards are more structured than the Major Arcana, divided into suits – cups, wands, swords and pentacles – with each suit representing a different practical aspect of what it means to be a human living in the world.

Cups represent our feelings and emotions, what they can tell us, how they can inspire us and how they influence our thoughts and behaviour.

Wands are about our energy, the drive that keeps us moving to fulfil our dreams and our soul's calling.

Swords represent the power of minds, our thoughts, our ideas and our beliefs. They hold the power to both empower and to hurt.

Pentacles represent our behaviour: what we actually do. They reflect our habits, our work, our choices and, through that, our identity.

The number of the card also holds some significance:

- **Aces** kick start new beginnings.

- **Twos** are about our choices and partnerships.

- **Threes** offer the safety of a grounding foundation.

- **Fours** show structures that can trap us or free us.

- **Fives** reflect our challenges and conflicts.

- **Sixes** are about growth through love.

- **Sevens** show us resilience, living in the real world.

- **Eights** encourage us to reflect and commit.

- **Nines** represent what we want and don't want.

- **Tens** show us climaxes and revelations that help us start again.

Lastly, each suit contains four court cards, each of which embodies some of the main characteristics of their suit:

- **Pages** are earnest beginners, still learning.

- **Knights** want to move and make things happen.

- **Queens** have learned inner confidence, wisdom and compassion.

- **Kings** know how to turn deep wisdom into action.

Refer back to these added, hidden meanings often to enhance your understanding of the cards.

Cups

Ace of Cups – Refill your cup

We get to begin again however many times we choose. Today is a new chance for you to be your best self and to seek out good things to 'fill your cup' with. How could you open more fully to what's around you? See what can you let flow in and flow out again. There is holiness here and real healing.

Keywords: opening, joy, flow, love, nourishment

Two of Cups – Ground love in truth

Relationships are an offering. We hope
someone will say a warm 'yes' to everything
we are, and in turn, we can choose to say that
same 'yes' back. Relationships hit problems
when we base our feelings on someone who
isn't really there. We can distort people in
our heads, only seeing what we wish for or
turning them into a projection of our fears and
insecurities. See the people in your life in their
true fullness and offer your real self in return.

Keywords: partnership, honesty

Three of Cups – Share joy

When life is stressful, we might find we
only turn toward people in our lives to
share woes. This card is an invitation to
pull your loved ones close and to let a
lightness break back into your conversations.
Celebrate what's going well! Today, really
notice the people you love and rekindle
that flush of affection and closeness.

Keywords: friendship, affection

Four of Cups – Notice what's offered

We can get so lost in our feelings, wallowing, complaining or trying to make things go our way, that we miss what's right in front of us. The world around you is always offering you full cups, messages and opportunities that could change the story you're ruminating on. Are you paying attention? Could you open and take what's being offered?

Keywords: discontent, apathy, rumination, negativity, excuse-making

Five of Cups – Hold on to what remains

Loss is one of the hardest feelings to bear. When something is truly gone or changed forever, nothing can be done. All our usual problem-solving tactics fail. We can only free-fall in the gap loss leaves and wait for the pain to ease. And yet…you are still here. See the two cups left behind you? Not everything is lost.

Keywords: loss, disappointment, heartache

Six of Cups – Look back with love

We can be so hard on our younger selves, over-inflating our mistakes or wishing things had been different. This card asks you to take on the role of the sweetest, most loving person you can imagine and then to look back at your past with this mindset. Without resentment, judgement or regret, what goodness can you find? The past often contains forgotten treasures.

Keywords: nostalgia, forgiveness, positivity

Seven of Cups – Root in reality

Thinking can be a real honey trap. In our heads, we can imagine anything we want, painting rosy pictures that only make us feel good, or proving ourselves right about how terrible something is by only focusing on what's wrong. It's all a mirage. In order to get what you need, you must come back to reality. Be courageous enough to find out what's actually true.

Keywords: delusion, bias, self-deception

Eight of Cups – Move on with faith

Turning away from something takes real courage. We know, deep down, when a situation doesn't hold what we need, but when it promises something soothing or easy instead, it can be tempting to ignore our needs and just settle. If there's something missing in your life, you're not going to find it by keeping everything the same. To seek the missing cup means picking a direction and moving on with no guarantees you'll get a better deal.

Keywords: passivity, stagnation, courage

Nine of Cups – Explore what really feels good

Are you chasing the right things? We all long to feel happy, but to feel genuine joy when good things happen, you need to have figured out what you actually want. Investigate what truly makes you happy every day; dig deep. Learn to get your heart, head and your behaviour authentically aligned to feel real contentment.

Keywords: peace, happiness, fulfilment

Ten of Cups – Enjoy where you are

We often imagine contentment as a 'when' scenario: I will be happy when I don't feel this, when I have that thing, when this isn't happening anymore. This card challenges our assumptions about 'happily ever after'. What if a good life is simply finding the sweetness in the here and now? Peace can arrive when we accept ourselves and all our feelings.

Keywords: gratitude, satisfaction, wholeness

Page of Cups – Open to possibility

It's easy to become jaded, to reduce everything to endless bad news or to add a cynical 'yeah, but.' Maybe it's a defence mechanism to protect us from feeling too much, but when we cut off our willingness to be surprised, we also cut off our creativity and our capacity to be inspired and to change. Connect to the childlike optimist inside you today.

Keywords: curiosity, creativity, openness

Knight of Cups – Keep sight of what's good for you

Ah, romance. Maybe you're getting swept away by an actual person, or it could be an irresistible idea, or any compulsion that makes you feel like throwing caution to the wind. Wild abandon is sometimes exactly what we need to get out of a rut, but this card also suggests caution. Look for evidence that your infatuation is good for you.

Keywords: infatuation, fantasy, risk

Queen of Cups – Tune into your feelings

Our culture often derides people for being 'too sensitive' but the Queen shows us that when we summon the strength to face our true feelings, we gain great power. Allowing ourselves to feel deeply grants us the ability to connect to and respond to the world around us. We can become a steady source of compassion, for ourselves and others.

Keywords: emotion, compassion, strength

King of Cups – Express what's true

If we can learn to feel our emotions deeply without getting swept away by them, we can start to find powerful ways to utilize those feelings. Today, see that emotions are nothing to be afraid of but are part of your wisdom. Look for opportunities to tap your emotional depths to create art, poetry, writing, or to be a teacher or leader.

Keywords: creativity, self-expression, groundedness, influence, wisdom

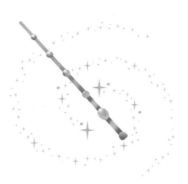

Wands

Ace of Wands – Nurture this new spark

Something new is alight in you. The nudge of a new idea? A growing passion or conviction? A 'maybe I could' goal or dream? Whatever it is, this card encourages you to take it seriously. It may still be just a tiny spark but, with time and attention, this new energy has the capacity to grow into something life-changing.

Keywords: inspiration, ideas, potential

Two of Wands – Choose something and commit

Do you have a choice to make? Are you hesitating, scared to commit to the wrong thing? Trying and failing isn't something to be afraid of. It's a far worse fate to live half-heartedly. If you're feeling disillusioned or let down by the reality of your life, see it as a chance to wake up.

Keywords: decisions, doubt, options, decisiveness, action

Three of Wands – Embrace life's potential

There is a wistfulness here. Threes have a stability to them, so first let's notice that you are standing on solid ground. Your life is full of good things. There's nothing wrong with wanting more. You could spend your whole life lethargically waiting, wishing. If you need a message to just do the thing, then this is it.

Keywords: ambition, potential, adventure

Four of Wands – Stop and celebrate

Celebration is a vital piece in the puzzle of how we learn how to feel happy. It reminds us of what's precious in our life, connects us with other people and lets us mark the passing of time. What could you celebrate? Today is a day to pause and savour. Find a way to mark life's changes.

Keywords: celebration, appreciation, ritual, acknowledgement, joy

Five of Wands – Don't waste your energy

Are you wrestling with something you don't like? Whether you lash out or stew quietly, there's a big 'don't want' mood about this card, a strong desire to get your own way to make things feel OK again. But is it getting you anywhere? Wands are all about energy. Don't lose yours to a stalemate, resenting and fighting things you can't control.

Keywords: conflict, tension, light-heartedness

Six of Wands – Enjoy your success

What does winning mean to you? Maybe you demand victory at all times, becoming defensive or broken by the slightest hint of criticism. On the other hand, maybe you feel unable to show pride in your accomplishments and nothing is ever good enough. This card challenges you to take a lighter, more joyful attitude toward winning. Celebrate all your achievements with good humour.

Keywords: success, victory, self-assurance, confidence, celebration

Seven of Wands – Don't give up

Does it feel like you versus the world? There's anger in this card and that's nothing to be afraid of. Anger is energy. It can show you what's important to you and help you defend what's precious. Let this energy help you to declare that enough is enough and drive you to make a change or seek some help. Gather your resolve and pick yourself up.

Keywords: courage, resolve, self-respect, challenges, resilience

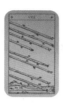

Eight of Wands – Follow the simplest path

We can spend our lives pushing against doors that won't open and miss the fact that there is an opening waiting for us somewhere else. This is the card of movement. It says to look for the open door, the clear way, somewhere there is space. Then start moving...GO!

Keywords: action, momentum, kick-start, flow, focus

Nine of Wands – Stay true to yourself

When we have good boundaries, we feel able to stay true to what is precious and meaningful to us. Boundaries are like your own personal code of conduct, something to help you live more authentically. These boundaries protect us from forces that try to turn us into something we don't want to be. What would be the bravest boundaries for you?

Keywords: boundaries, conviction, integrity

Ten of Wands – Lighten your load

The heaviest card. Our lives feel too much to bear some days but we put our heads down and trudge on. Let's stop and look at these sticks of yours. Have you taken on more than your share? Ten marks the end of a cycle so there is hope. You could put some of these sticks down or ask for help. Think about your boundaries today.

Keywords: burden, overwhelm, responsibility, martyrdom, imbalance

Page of Wands – Start and see what happens

When inspiration strikes, it feels like waking up. Suddenly, something new feels possible. Maybe everything feels possible. Don't let anyone try to squash this feeling in you. Seek out people who will encourage you. You need to do something to get this ball rolling – don't keep it all in your head. Take the smallest seed of possibility and run with it.

Keywords: vision, creativity, beginner

Knight of Wands – Hold your nerve

To change things we have to uproot ourselves from solid ground and lean into what's unsteady and uncertain. The runaway-horse energy in this card reflects how that can feel both exhilarating and frightening. You're not entirely in control, but maybe that's what's needed to get you somewhere new? Today, don't be put off by that adrenaline surge as things shift around you.

Keywords: impulsiveness, risk, excitement

Queen of Wands – Protect and nurture positive energy

There is a kind of fire that feeds us, warms us and welcomes others; a slow, steady, productive sort of flame that we must keep tending to, to keep it burning. What fuels this kind of energy in you? It might be creativity, caring for others, nature. What threatens to put this fire out? How could you better protect and feed this good fire?

Keywords: willpower, strength, warmth

King of Wands – Use rebellion
for good

Think heat, ignition, red and strong, the kind that makes things happen. This kind of intensity can change the world, for good and for ill. Its bold impulsivity stirs up the status quo and breaks all the rules. It's time to see your energy and take responsibility. How could you better ignite and wield this force within you? What change could it fuel, what could it burn away and what could it reveal?

Keywords: intensity, passion, rebellion, vision, charisma

Swords

Ace of Swords – Stop deliberating

This ace marks the opportunity to embrace a new, decisive way of thinking. Maybe you've been feeling confused or muddled, trying to hold too many ideas or truths at once, or you're resisting 'picking a side.' This card says: make a decision about what's right and true, and act. You can always change your mind as you go.

Keywords: clarity, breakthrough, action

Two of Swords – Look at the evidence

Making a good choice is about choosing the most helpful things to focus on. When something overwhelms you but you know you must make a choice, lay out all your evidence, thoughts and interpretations. Which story makes you feel strong? Which thoughts keep you stuck and miserable? Reinforce the good thoughts and the right choice becomes much more obvious.

Keywords: decisions, stalemate, blocks

Three of Swords – Be honest about how you feel

We can't think or avoid our way out of pain. Sometimes life simply pierces us. This is the pain of heartbreak, of profound grief, deep hurt. The relief in this card is that it says: don't cover anything up or power through. In order to move through us and not get stuck, feelings need to be felt and expressed. You are allowed to be vulnerable and to have needs.

Keywords: heartbreak, pain, wounds, release

Four of Swords – Rest your mind

A society obsessed with productivity and self-improvement puts us under a lot of pressure to be on the go all the time. This card is a firm hand on your shoulder telling you to stop. It's not just our bodies that need rest, it's our minds. When you're resting, are you really resting? True rest – actually putting everything down – can feel uncomfortable or scary, but it's in these still moments that we most often find sudden clarity and insight.

Keywords: rest, stillness, restoration

Five of Swords – Take responsibility

There's a real sense of conflict in this card. Do you feel like the justified victor? Or do you feel like you've been treated unfairly? This card can be a good encouragement to watch how your thoughts and words are escalating the situation. What are the plain facts? Whether you feel righteous or wretched, remember you have choices. You can decide to change the story.

Keywords: conflict, bitterness, blame, choice

Six of Swords – Don't wait to feel ready

We often wait to 'feel ready' when we know that change is going to hurt or when we feel that we're not good enough as the person we are right now. This card invites you to pick up your baggage, your wounds and your fears, exactly as you are, and start anyway. Who knows what's on the other side of this?

Keywords: change, transition, recovery, hope

Seven of Swords – Be honest with yourself

The card of betrayal. Other people let us down in life: they lie, cheat and hurt. But it can be far easier to point fingers of blame than to admit that we don't always act well either. Today, think about authenticity. Do your actions match your values and promises? Are you using half-truths to control the narrative or to cover something up?

Keywords: deception, betrayal, self-honesty

Eight of Swords – Don't jump to conclusions

We can end up stuck when we believe in one 'right' way to do things but can't seem to live up to that ideal, when we believe that taking action is going to make us feel something we don't like, and when we repeatedly tell ourselves stories about who we are and what things mean. The key to this card is remembering that beliefs are thoughts, not reality. Take the blindfold off.

Keywords: restriction, helplessness, rumination

Nine of Swords – Remember this isn't the end

A card of nightmares; the kind of mental anguish that feels like the end of everything. But what if this isn't the end of the story? Do anything but sit there in the dark playing it over in your mind. Get up. There is plenty of room here yet for things to play out in ways you can't predict.

Keywords: despair, distress, panic, rumination, self-sabotage

Page of Swords – Check your blind spots

Passion can be wonderful, but now might be a good time to check in. Are you using your ideas and opinions to inspire others, or to try and control everything? Endlessly defending our thoughts and opinions can lead us to have a very cloudy view of things. Can you release the tight hold you have on everything just a little to help you see things more clearly?

Keywords: passion, enthusiasm, defensiveness

Ten of Swords – Turn toward healing

Ouch. Remember that swords represent your mind, so even though you may feel pierced through, you are safe in this moment. This intensity will pass. More hopeful still – Tens signify an ending. You might have been hurt or frightened, deeply, but it's done. So what next? Next you start the bloody, slow business of pulling out those swords, one at a time, and healing your wounds.

Keywords: defeat, endings, pain, healing

Knight of Swords – Practise focus

Modern life actively discourages us from commitment. Instead, it encourages us to rush, multi-task, to instantly swap out anything that feels uncomfortable for something better and to constantly search for something new to entertain or soothe us. Single-pointed focus is a kind of superpower: it gives you an edge. What in your life would benefit from this kind of focus?

Keywords: single-mindedness, commitment, determination, focus, action

Queen of Swords – Examine 'truth'

The truth is often more complex than we imagine. When we feel insecure, we can get pulled back into that childish part of us that judges and clings to absolutes, but the Queen represents that older, self-assured, calm part of you that values wisdom over winning. If you can cut away what's delusional, unhelpful or untrue, you can hold real power to change your life and do good.

Keywords: clarity, independence, wisdom

King of Swords – Notice what has your attention

Where's your head at? It's a matter of life or death because what you focus on moment to moment will decide what lives, what grows and what dies. The way to feed something is to give it attention. The way to kill something is to turn away from it. If you can learn to see what you're actually doing, with discernment and responsibility, you will shape the life you most want.

Keywords: focus, insight, responsibility

Pentacles

Ace of Pentacles – Say 'yes'

All great changes start with noticing that we're being offered something. The world might be offering you a new insight or vision, some time or spare cash, someone to help – it could be anything. If you're hoping to make a change or to start something new, keep your eyes open for what resources and possibilities are all around you today.

Keywords: opportunity, gifts, abundance, support, change

Two of Pentacles – Don't take anything too seriously

When there's a lot to think about or do, we can feel wrung out and overwhelmed, even self-pitying. We forget that being busy offers a wonderful opportunity to be playful and to enjoy being alive. What could you learn from the juggler? To bend and flex, balance, laugh and have fun.

Keywords: busyness, flexibility, priorities, energy, balance

Three of Pentacles – Invite others to join you

When we try to do everything on our own, our path gets very dark and narrow. When we connect with others, we find light and space. Maybe there you'll learn something new, or maybe you'll act as a catalyst in someone else's journey. What happens if you stop seeing your dreams and ambitions as a solo affair?

Keywords: collaboration, teamwork, synergy

Four of Pentacles – Trust in abundance

We often feel stuck when we believe that there isn't enough to go around: enough money, success, luck, love. We obsess over what we're lacking or might lose and feel resentful of others if they get something first. What if the way to access it was to open up and be more generous? Be brave: give away some of what feels scarce in your life and see what happens.

Keywords: hoarding, resentment, fear, trust

Five of Pentacles – Let in the good

Feeling like you've lost everything can freeze you solid. When something bad happens, you might tell yourself that you don't deserve good things, that you're being punished, that you're broken, unwelcome and irredeemable, so you stay where you are, stuck in the cold and the dark. But what if you didn't need to stay frozen and hungry? You are always welcome to step back into life.

Keywords: loss, suffering, hardship

Six of Pentacles – Explore reciprocity

The idea of giving and receiving is complex. We can give or receive with no expectations or strings attached, or it can come with a deeper agenda. Are you more the giver or the receiver? Today, think about what lies underneath that dynamic. Are you giving but resenting it? Receiving but feeling squashed?

Keywords: relationships, reciprocation, power

Seven of Pentacles – Notice what's going well

This is an invitation to rest and reflect on how well things are going. Are things, actually, just fine? This is a good chance to challenge your attitude of 'never enough' and take some time for gratitude. Even if you do need to alter course, it's no big deal. Just look at your patterns and habits with compassion for clues about what to work on next.

Keywords: reward, satisfaction, contentment

Eight of Pentacles – Commit to showing up

How often do you manage to settle down and do real work on things that matter to you? If you're attempting any kind of regular practice, you'll know how hard it is. It's important to work out what's getting in the way. Often it's perfectionism and a fear of failing. We set the bar so high that we freeze up under the pressure. But progress only comes if you actually show up and do the work.

Keywords: commitment, repetition, practise

Nine of Pentacles – Invest in your future

Gardens remind us that for growth, we must water, prune, weed, try again. When the harvest comes, we pause and appreciate our reward. So is your life right now feeling barren? Think seeds, patience and commitment. If you see that things around you are actually quite comfortable and full, what could you pick and enjoy?

Keywords: abundance, reward, pleasure

Ten of Pentacles – Celebrate your interconnection

Today, remember that you belong. You belong to yourself, to your body, to people around you, to your neighbourhood, to the wider world, the trees, the birds, the flowers. This is a day to see and celebrate your interconnectedness. What overlooked relationship could you deepen and grow?

Keywords: connection, community

Page of Pentacles – Learning

Studying something is a kind of devotion: a way for us to honour that life is rich and interesting and that we don't know everything. When you decide to learn, you have a chance to open your heart as well as your mind, to expand your understanding of the world and yourself. How could you embrace the deeper attitude of a student today? What could it inspire you to do?

Keywords: learning, openness, practise, study

Knight of Pentacles – Hold your course

Because it's normal for our minds to race and our emotions to fluctuate, it can be hard to stay steady. In order to get anywhere, sometimes we need to turn away from drama and just get on with it. This card is a challenge to simply knuckle down and work hard until the work is done. The energy here is slow but determined.

Keywords: consistency, focus, dedication

Queen of Pentacles – Give with confidence

Once we understand that there's more than enough goodness to go around and that we can create our happiness no matter what, we gain the freedom and strength to become truly generous rather than self-protective. Today, turn toward the world and people around you and practise what you know to be right.

Keywords: self-sufficiency, generosity

King of Pentacles – Focus on practical next steps

The idea of taking responsibility can feel heavy, but what if you thought of it as a kind of power? Life is fundamentally unpredictable. You can't control what each day brings, but you can choose what you're going to do next. By focusing on your own actions, your life becomes something you can craft, moment to moment, rather than something that just happens to you.

Keywords: responsibility, power, leadership, agency, independence

Card Spreads
and Stories

Once the cards start to feel like familiar friends, you might like to introduce spread into your practice. A Tarot spread is just a way of laying out multiple cards in a particular pattern in order to weave multiple card meanings together. There are a number of traditional spreads that you'll see used in Tarot examples, such as the Celtic Cross, but there are no official ways of laying out the cards and no particular spread is needed to make the cards 'work' better. Being inventive with Tarot spreads is one of the best ways to introduce creativity into your practice and make it your own.

What to Do

Start by choosing one area of your life or a specific situation you'd like to explore. Perhaps it's something you're worried about, or a relationship or some aspect of your work or career – just whatever you'd like more clarity on. Then, in the same way that you'd pick your daily card (see page 15), pick out the number of cards that you'd like to work with and lay them out in front of you.

Two-Card Spreads

The simplest and most natural evolution from a one-card draw is two cards! Introducing the extra dynamic of a second card is the perfect way to broaden your understanding of a situation and add additional context and clues. What two different aspects of your experience, thoughts, behaviour or difficulty could you explore? Maybe your two-card story could look something like this. Just choose one set or pair from the list to start with, then with your eyes closed, pick out one card from your deck for each aspect. What other pairs can you think of?

The first card you draw	The second card you draw
The surface situation	The deeper truth
Now	Next
Me	Another person
Where I am	What I'm missing
One choice available to me	A second choice
My strengths	My blind spots
What I know	What I need to learn
What I think is happening	What is actually happening

Three-Card Spreads

Here we have the chance to add an additional 'plot
point.' Can you see how each additional card adds a
new layer of story?

Again, decide in advance which story 'triplet' you'd
like to explore or write your own, close your eyes
and pick your cards.

First card	Second card	Third card
Where I've come from	Where am I	Where I'm headed
What's happening	What's getting in the way	Where I need to be
What I'm doing well	What isn't working	How I need to change
What I'm thinking about	What I'm doing	The consequence
What I want	What I need	What I need to be careful of
Influences from the past	Influences in the present	The teacher I need next
Who I was	Who I am now	Who I could be
Me	Another person	What unites us

Spread Shapes and Patterns

Three-card spreads are a good opportunity to start bringing in a sense of shape and design to your story spread. Think about the examples above and consider how you could place your three cards on the table in front of you.

- Do they follow an order through time like a line?

- Perhaps you'd like to lay them out like a triangle that leads the story round in a circle.

- You might like to lay out two cards with one that acts as the obstacle or wall between them.

- Maybe your three cards could be like a staircase climbing toward something higher.

- Does one card 'dominate' the others, rising over them?

- Or is there a hidden influence that lies below the others?

There are no wrong answers here. What makes sense to you? What would best illustrate the story you are exploring?

You might like to design your spread in advance, drawing your design on a piece of paper to lay your cards over as you pull them from the deck. Or you could lay out the cards first and see what shape they seem to lend themselves to as you explore their meanings. Keep track of your designs and story questions in your notebook so that you can use them again or refine them in the future.

As you get more confident, you can experiment with four, five and six card spreads...or even more! Four-card spreads lend themselves nicely to a balanced square, five to a star or flower shape, and six cards to a hierarchical pyramid in a 3-2-1 arrangement. With your situation in mind, you could even think of laying out multiple cards like the panels of a graphic novel and 'reading' them like a comic book. You could lay out one card for each day of the week in advance and see how/if that story plays out, or the same for the months of a new year. The possibilities really are endless so have fun with it.

An Example Reading Using Spreads

Let's say that I had a conversation with a friend yesterday that has left me feeling insecure. I'm not sure why – she didn't say anything hurtful – but something about the interaction is playing on my mind and I feel raw and small. What three aspects of the situation might help me gain some insight into how I'm feeling?

We could try:

- My reality

- My friend's reality

- The thought that's getting in the way of me seeing clearly

I'll draw three cards, focusing on each of these aspects in turn, placing the 'thought' card between me and my friend to symbolize the obstruction. What story do the cards tell?

My reality	**The thought that's getting in the way of me seeing clearly**	**My friend's reality**

The Emperor	**Seven of Cups**	**King of Wands**
I'm having to be very strong in my life and shoulder a great deal of responsibility	I wish things could be different for me. It's not fair – it's all so easy for her. If only I was more like her, my life would be better	My friend is full of energy, charisma and drive. People are drawn to her and she's receiving a lot of praise and attention

Yes, that feels true. Now, I'll redraw and replace the middle card, asking: What perspective could help me feel better?

I love the three strong figures that complete our spread! Wishful thinking, resentment and comparison were warping my perspective. I see now that I am my own kind of leader: one who's quietly creating a better life for myself day by day. I can feel proud of my strength and courage.

My reality	What perspective could help me feel better?	My friend's reality

The Emperor	**King of Pentacles**	**King of Wands**
I'm having to be very strong in my life and shoulder a great deal of responsibility	Maybe my actions aren't so visible to others, but I hold a different kind of power. I can keep making good choices and steer my life in a positive direction	My friend is full of energy, charisma and drive. People are drawn to her and she's receiving a lot of praise and attention

Tarot in
Everyday Life

My hope is that Tarot can be a companion to you.
A consistent anchor and sanctuary that can bring
a real sense of support to your life. But your daily
Tarot reading is just the beginning. Here are some
more ways you can weave the cards into your way of
living and seeing.

Tarot Shrines and Talismans

If one particular card seems to resonate with you
more deeply, especially if you find it keeps coming
up in your readings, why not find ways to bring it
into the wider world with you? You could set aside a
place on a shelf dedicated to your card and begin to
collect and gather things to represent it, or pick one
small thing to carry around with you. What objects
come to mind? Any colours? What key words? What
about animals or plants? Draw things, find, make.

Elements

Many of the cards, particularly in the Minor
Arcana, have an element associated with them.
Cups speak to water, wands to fire, swords to air
and pentacles to Earth. Each day that you draw
a card, look for the element within it and then
make time to connect to that element in your
surroundings that day, using all of your senses.

Art and Writing

Tarot cards can be a wonderful catalyst for creative work. Perhaps you'd like to try and draw or paint your own version of your daily card, in an abstract or figurative style. You could write about the characters and the situation you see within a card, like looking through a window into another world. See each card as a deep pool. How could you dive in with your imagination? What could you draw back out to show the world?

Reading for Other People

If Tarot really gets under your skin and starts to become a part of your life, it is natural to begin thinking about doing readings for other people. If your friends and family know that you use Tarot cards, they might even ask you directly if you will read for them.

If this is something you'd like to consider, please do take the following thoughts to heart.

Tarot touches on some of our deepest human wounds, dysfunctions and psychology. Just as counsellors and psychologists must train to help people face their darkness and joys with skill, Tarot readers also have a responsibility to handle others with training and care. Remember that your interpretations of the cards could have a big impact on someone's mood, sense of safety, hope and behaviour. Tread carefully. Perhaps Tarot could be a wonderful accompaniment to an additional therapeutic practice you may like to train in.

All people have the ability to read Tarot for themselves and draw their own insights. Rather than telling people what their cards mean, how could you help others build their own relationship with the cards? Perhaps a reading is something you could do together, sharing ideas and lending your understanding, rather than a message you deliver.

Before reading for others, I would encourage you to study Tarot in depth and to take your time. Read widely, both classic Tarot texts and new. Tarot is a rich tradition and it's evolving all the time. Rather than simply memorizing and repeating other people's interpretations or approaches, how could you bring your own wisdom to a reading? You have something unique and valuable to add to Tarot's potential.

Also available

the little book of
Inner Peace

Ashley Davis Bush

the little book of
Mindfulness

Dr Patrizia Collard

the little book of
Gratitude

Dr Robert A Emmons

the little book of
Meditation

Dr Patrizia Collard

the little book of
Shadow Work

Richard Martyn